the name of this book is untitled but that's a bit of a lie

I0472920

Morgan Drolet

and

Shawn Sullivan

NEON BURRITO PUBLISHING

◀2◁

cover photo: Karl Kendrick Kellawan the Third

Gus: the cat

Morgan Christopher Drolet

Born in California. Microwaved eggs.

Shawn Michael Sullivan

Didn't expect this to happen.

XXVII

I looked at a picture of you as a child
Blond hair with dark roots
Even as I've seen it
With your smile posed in front of a white
picket fence
I wonder what's in that smile
What happened to you that day
Was your mom
Off to the side of the camera
Watching
The smile looks real enough
You look like a happy kid
But I know times were tough
Back then
Back when your dad left
When that pain was still raw
Each day must have been confusing as hell
Maybe all your actions still owe themselves to
those wounds
I don't like to ask you about it
And I forget sometimes
And I'm a little afraid
And sometimes I feel a quiet sadness
Like today
When I looked at that picture
And wondered about you back then

XXVIII

A middle aged woman in a
Pantsuit
Mary according to the sign
In front of a flower shop
Her arm gingerly outstretched
Trying to stay up wind
Turns spray paints silver the clipped fronds
Off some green tropical behemoth
Lookin like pancaked reptile paws
All dressed up for the holidays

XXVIV

A young homeless Arab in worn socks
lying on the ground
howling clapping
Shaking snakes of oil black hair
Saturated sucking
Sweat
Cheeks exploding imploding
It's an ambitious Louis Armstrong
impersonation
Humming acid daydreams
The policeman standing above claps on the
off beats
The muted thwack of his polypropylene
gloves
Saturated
Baby blue
The shutter sing blades of sky above his face

XXX

because of my emotions
being like weather
i find the most comfort on clear and warm
days

los angeles
i'd heard of its 72-and-sunny before i arrived
with the kinda goal in me
a vintage dream that i hope endures

to internalize los angeles
including, neon from nights
since nights i like most, actually

XXXI

this is a secret to my writing that i should
keep to myself:

i pace around like a maniac thinking about
how i want to write
what it feels like to want to write
what it feels like to be feeling

i become lost from the topic of what i was
writing
waste time on myself, wonder about myself
work on myself, work on my adult reputation
when necessary, indeed i also
perform work that improves my adult
reputation
then i remember again how i want to write
and i think about what i want to write

then i realize i'm hungry so i go eat a burrito
i drink caffeine i walk to the 3rd street cvs
buy a candy bar, i eat the candy bar
while spinning blocks back to my apartment

XXXII

4pm Christmas Eve
Downtown the streets are warm and blank as
a map
The scene is reminiscent of those early
mornings
Wandering through themed Vegas casinos
Their indoor scale buildings and painted sky's
Soundless save the distant whir of a motor
around some corner
I keep putting off the grocery store and its
interminable lines
Where I want to buy a steak for dinner and
leftover breakfast
Beautiful men and women will rain down on
shimmering parties
  tonight
Drinking and laughing on credit
Which will be collected in the morning
Tonight
Transvestites will paint their faces with
Holliday glow
That may leak off by sunrise
In hollywood the bums in their Santa hats
Red as their faces and just as bruised

Will clang bottles and smoke their Christmas
trees down to yellow fingertips
And I stand
Looking out the turret window of my corner
apartment
Wondering where to go from here

XXXIII

a poem that's a quiet room

with no worries about a clock
and

all those roars outside the room
are imaginary, they don't exist here

to truly be a quiet room
i'll try being quiet to myself because
i scream at myself regularly

so often
later i will again
when i read this. i'll think to myself
"why'd i do this??"
which is the mantra of my life's reflections

[omitted section that said, for example:
this poem is being written past midnight
christmas eve
brett is visiting family in san diego
i'm in a quiet room to write my quiet poem]

XXXIV

His life was like throwing out canvass starting
pleased with the progression so pleased he
found it hard to continue after a point For
fear of ruining what had gone so smoothly
Then pushing forward into a snag Trying
every way to posh through Before discarding
the work and starting anew
She thought about her life as a picture of a
galaxy
Looking thin and splatters
Easily blown awayable
Taken from a million miles away
Through a telescope
Again
Thin and small by scale
But huge when you got right up to it
Unfathomable and unattainable
Full of wandering vessels she couldn't dream
Full and huge
Endless from the inside
Until the knowledge of its edges became
reality

XXXV

this poem happens:

when i'm processing all the things
i've done in a day, and people i've seen

and what i did and who i was
and what that means, and i chew my errors

the thing i try to remember is
i can't regret what hasn't happened
and the worst part would be
not making anything happen at all

XXXVI

She fiddled with her phone
The other hand methodical
Unlacing the rows of tightly packed braids
Massaging the scalp
Beginning on another braid
The massaging must have felt
The way it does
Running a hand through brittle
Matted hair that's been
Crushed motionless by an all day hat
Every so often
At abrupt interval
The woman behind would lapse into a
murmur of tears

XXXVII

Old man juggling a bike looking through a wonders
of the world calendar
Getting to the end and starting again
The same 12
Maybe 13 pictures over and over
He's planing his past in expired boxes
Headlined with lush or desolate expanses
Meanwhile just behind him
Young and black but balding
With a picked out fro atop an ever lengthening
forehead
He's got a red backpack and a box of hazelnut
creamer
Left hand clutching a Spanish onion
The tail of the onion begins to shake
It's a lizard
Opening the box
Reptilian necks begin to crane
Bulging eyes
He shoves the onetime onion ne lizard
No he sets it delicately
In to the dark of the box with its comrades
I notice now
For the first time the one
On his backpack
Nearly glowing green leviathan
Judiciously taking in the calendar thrills
From his perch behind the cyclists shoulder
 And me
 A fly on the wall

XXXVIII

most of my happiness
doesn't come from the world
because the world
doesn't operate on my happiness
a recurring flaw of mine
is acting like an emotional victim

XXXIX

There's the bible then there's me
I'm the fourth God
shut up devil shut up when I'm talking
Tell the truth says the devil
tell me about the number seven
Tell me about the Devils you know
The Devils you've got inside you
Shut up devil shut up when I'm preachin
The bus slowed to a halt
One passenger shouted
Call the police
Then another
Then the same woman again
The driver asked for quiet over the microphone
God and the devil were silent
The bus began to hit its stride once more
Undulating
humming hot with the breath of bodies
God screamed over his radio
Into his radio
Get your butt outta my face
Don't stand so close to me
The devil smiled and bit an apple
Tell me fourth god
He's chewing now
about the number seven
God screamed and rocketed from his seat
His Ox-blood jacket shook with rage
Eyes looked strangled and framed with pain

Cracked black hands
Clench splay clench
The devil stood
Yanking the yellow rope
as the bus came to stop
Merry Christmas he says
no one is dying
 And the devil exits the bus
Merry Christmas said God no. 4
I love you guys
 And God was silent

XL

this is an entire fucking goddamn trilogy about
working at a book store the
day before christmas eve:

a
the woman waiting for someone to finish making her
drink
i see her crying
i have no idea why she's crying
she's just crying
without making a spectacle

i feel like i can relate to her waiting for her drink
with tears
she's a symbol of my feelings about life

b
a red hoodie and black-rimmed glasses and
mascara around her eyes and black hair and
i see a part of myself in
the personality of her eyes
something dark and vicious
brown eyes
anyway

she's come to me and said
she has a list of books she wants me to find
i look at her phone and see dale carnegie's
how to win friends & influence people, which is a
classic

in the self-improvement area, a classic

without even scanning the rest of her list
i'm snotty with her
about looking up her five or so books
i ask her if she needs me to look all of them up

she says yes
she'd like me to look up the entire list

i give her a pen and paper and tell her to write down
the titles
i tell her i'll be back
i head into a section and put some books away
i take a minute

i come back and she's written a couple titles
at the top of the page
in blue ink
she's written
how to win friends & influence people
"ohhhhk" i say, real snotty
and we head out together into the self-improvement
area

how to win friends & influence people isn't there in
paperback
there's a hardcover, i mention there's usually a
paperback
i mention paperback is cheaper
i look at her for a moment
she's standing there
we go through the list and a couple books aren't in
stock
one i have to look for it in a different section

i apologize to her for when i was being rude
or annoyed or irritated or, whatever

i say it
i say i appreciate how mellow she is

she stayed mellow
so we both became mellow
she was a bit of hero to me

c
he's a kinda crotchety 25 year-old
tends to complain about things
hates doing things
works a full week of hours
works in all the storer's departments
works a lot and hates it and keeps going

he comes from third floor and gives me a paper
we chat for a second as he descends to first floor
then i look at the paper
with curiosity

on his way through my floor to the third, i ask him
what he gave me the paper for
he says a manager told him to give it to second floor
and i should get the book and call the person

i find the book and wonder about
the procedure for phone payment
i bring the book upstairs
i can't talk to a manager
because there's a manager meeting
i notice the guy from earlier, idly chatting with
another coworker

i hold the paper out to him and tell him to take it
he laughs, he looks at our coworker
the coworker makes "a face" and turns away
i remind him he brought me the paper

he shakes his head and laughs
i tell him "i hate how you're laughing at me"
the other co-worker leaves

i say "i'll remember this" while holding out the paper
the paper in his hand, he says "i bet you will"
and i say "oh i will" while walking away

i head to second floor i'm shelving books
from a cart he'd been working on earlier
he comes down and we chat, normal chat
then he heads to first floor

but the big moment comes later
about an hour later, when he's on his way upstairs
and asks me if i'd been upset earlier

i stick my hand out to him
he says something else
i mention my hand
he shakes his head
he shakes my hand

he says something like "because i'm sorry if
earlier..."
i confess to him i also think it's odd i'd gotten upset
i call myself "fragile" today
he makes an "i didn't know if..." comment
i tell him i've already forgiven him

anyway secretly i was glad he'd been stuck with the
paper situation

XLI

thing is, poetry has a bit of a personal problem
a bad reputation
poetry is a total rockabilly nogood greaser

and rockabilly is a keyword for a search engine
in the days of the tech world

the past is a dumpster
i've always found dumpster divers fascinating

XLII

I rode into the city
Arcing up and over the moat surrounding
It seemed to be a gangway
Boarding me onto a great steel vessel
Anchored on the blackening sea
The grey sky brushed breadcrumbs of rain from its
table
The streets raged
With waitresses and stockbrokers and jewelers and
cops and transient acoustic minstrels
In the alleys
And
Down
The steel streets with their masts of glass monolithic
chambers
The dust and smoke blossoms
The city's breath sings past
Like the Mistral through the windows of the chateau
d'If

XLIII

it's easy for me to find another depressive
conversationalist
because many sociopaths
carry a bizarre longing to be listened to
and to debate who currently has the most right to be
upset
or agree on all the reasons to be upset

ready to be
upset any day, any moment
ready to talk about it
ready to overexplain, overstory, overapologize

a non-conversationalist hears
blah-blah-blah
doesn't wanna hear anyone else's story at all
doesn't wanna tell their own

though i think everyone's got a big ol' conversation
going on within themselves

non-conversationalists have the good idea of being
quiet about everything
they put their problems on mute
they don't speak until spoken to
then they say maybe there doesn't need to be so
much speaking

i like quiet times with quiet people
i like loud moments with loud people
and i think that either way
we're all just trying our best

XLIV

down people battling longtime blues
wanna know
who's got the best sass

in an ultimate sense
the best sass is the same as the best of anything
the best last forever

in a daily sense
it's the sound of the sass
hard sass on the right person, in the right moment
when the person was making the wrong thing
happen
that's so fucking chill

XLV

you've maybe read another poem of mine
or seen something of mine from cameras
or examined my tinder or instragram
texted me, maybe
listened to my favorite songs
they're your favorite songs too
we share the same favorite food!
you think you got the jist of me

but when you meet me
face to face
on a day not connected with another day
you'll always be one story behind

because the things that make me feel better aren't
always there
+ the things that hurt me come from wherever
whenever they want

i'm a man of emotions and impulses
with mistakes from my emotions and impulses
which later, when i realize the mistakes, if i do, will
make me emotional
and i'll probably do something impulsive
to make up for my previous impulse
i can here and there make a good decision
but, for reasons i can't explain
effects of the good tend to linger for less time than
the bad

so what lifts me up can only lift me for so long

and what crushes me crushes me

knowing the total me, the real me
requires knowing me day by day

might not be worth it, tbh
it's like wandering the beach with a metal detector
a true analogy, for sure, because that's how i feel
about myself
and i'm searching for, like, a long-lost ww2
submarine
even though ww2 didn't happen here
even though the beach is crowded with other people
even though my plan is terrible and unfactual
my buttoned-up shirt has a tacky parrot theme
my shirt doesn't blend with my pastel shorts
it looks like i have a wicker basket on my head

XLVI

I'm slowly stirring Kraft Italian dressing into a bowl
of microwaved frozen corn
There is an empty carton of eggs being
Used as a paper weight
On a stack of ripening bills
We are $783.44 late to Edison
I microwaved the corn too long and the skin has
shriveled like a nut sack
Someone has used the water bill to light a candle
The mismatched lampshades throw bent shadows
mimicking winking eye
Having eaten and smoked a joint
I settle in to
Shit
I forgot my coffee
Here we are
I light a cigarette and settle
Into this sinking couch
With its fabric patterns of bus seat replica design
And crack the spine
Shit
Wheres that fucking ashtray?
Ah
And crack the spine on Anna Seghers
The smoke clinging to the wall sconces
Echoing the mist around the moon

XLVII

anne rice, stephen king
them most of all
because i think h.p. lovecraft and edgar allen poe are
better writers

so i'm talking about the ones who people get nasty
about
those who aren't doing their art right
according to those who wanna be in the know

you don't even realize what you're doing, do you,
critical crowd
you're making them better, truer
by reminding the readers that darkness will always
be around

XLVIII

We watched papillon in the couch and smoked a joint
We fucked in my bed
And after
I lay next to you thinking
"Hey you bastards, I'm still here"
We ate oatmeal cookies my mom had sent for
Christmas
The band bleeding their basement farmhouse fervor
all around us through the stereo
I drank coffee from a red cup
Gilded peacocks and dragons perched on hot clouds
in the enamel
You drank tea
Throat raw from the dry cold of the past couple
weeks
We walked through the rooms
Of my small apartment
Our heavy heels whomping the floorboards
I wrapped your mothers gift with brown paper lunch
bags
The way we did in school
We kissed goodnight
You going back to your mom in the valley
Me going back to a book

THIS BOOK ALREADY ENDED